To LaNell —

For all the nice

things you do — with love

Alice

The back step is a special spot,
impromptu seating for adult and tot.
> *Hurrah for the back step!*

A gathering place for two or three,
or a relaxing stop for only me
> here on the back step.

No need to go and get a chair,
let's just sit here
> *on the back step.*

ON THE BACK STEP

Doris Stensland

ON THE BACK STEP
© by Doris Stensland 1998

Library of Congress
Catalog Card Number: 98-90832

ISBN: 1-880552-04-3

Stensland Publications
47897 290th Street
Canton, South Dakota 57013

Printed in the United States of America

PINE HILL PRESS, INC.

Freeman, S. Dak. 57029

Dedicated to my husband, Hans,
who with love and encouragement
has made it possible for me to follow
my dreams.

CONTENTS

Country Days
1

Nature Entertains
23

Family . . . and Other People
41

Special Days
65

Unto Thee, O Lord, Do I Lift Up My Voice
91

Conversations with Eve
135

COUNTRY DAYS

ON THE BACK STOOP

Sitting on the back step
in late afternoon
is an enchanting way to
punctuate my day. I relax
and let nature entertain
and inspire me. Soft twilight sounds calm
my ruffled nerves and as I
take in the immense dimensions
of God's world, my petty problems
shrink in size.
Butterflies flutter here and there,
and there's no rhyme or reason
to their goings,
But birds fly home to nest
and join together
in evening twitterings.
A familiar step comes up
the walk to meet me
there.
And together we watch
the little hummingbird make its last rounds
of the merry red petunias, and as it
briefly lingers, extracting each
last drop,
it seems to say,
*"This time of day produces the
sweetest nectars."*

COUNTRY GIRL

She takes each day
and pockets it
for future use.
A lark's sweet tune
replayed
may one day cheer
her troubled heart
and make it sing.
And when her world
is cold and stiff
she'll think
of lambs pirouetting
at their play
and she will smile.

OLD-FASHIONED THRESHING DAYS

It was a different time,
another era,
the high point of the agricultural year
when the sun was high
and its rays beat down
on land and man and beast.

Then it was time
for the threshing machine
to chug into the farmyard
with teams of horses and hayracks
in happy procession.
The golden shocks of grain
which had so nicely decorated
the fields
would soon be lifted
one by one
by hard-working, sweat-soaked men
into the waiting hayracks
and then tossed into the big machine
to erupt as golden grain
and a shiny straw stack.

It was a different time,
another era,
before air conditioning
or electric stoves
when women helped each other
feed these hungry workers.
All day they stood over hot stoves
fueled with corn cobs

with sweat trickling down their cheeks
as they baked pies and cakes,
fried chicken and meat
and prepared the nourishing farm food
for meals and lunches.

It was a different time,
another era
which now exists only in our memories,
when work was a special event
and camaraderie made the event
a festivity.

"It's Irrelevant"

Little black lamb,
as you skip and you leap,
Do you care that you're different
from other sheep?

I wonder, have you ever been teased
for being dark and dusky-fleeced?
Or did you ever stop and cry
because the white sheep passed you by?

It answered, while doing a happy pirouette,
"Does it matter to you if you're blond or brunette?"

TREATISE ON TAILS

Tails were made for days like these,
when flies molest and mosquitoes tease.
For swinging action, they're a dandy,
(The cow's flyswatter is always handy.)
But it's hard for the farmer
to hold his tongue
When a dirty tail in his face is flung!

LASSIE WITH THE HAPPY HEART

Tresses like the ripened wheat,
apple-blossom skin;
the quiet beauty of a dawn
whose daintiness steals
on the scene.
She moves with litheness as
a doe,
is friend of sun and breeze.
Her exhubrance splashes
like a stream
a-tumbling over rock and stone.

Oh, lassie with the happy heart,
indelibly inscribed
with music of a thousand larks
bright sunsets
lambs at play.
Today you walk on country lanes
where violets and clover bloom,
But even though some day you step
on concrete paths in busy towns,
still life can never more erase
these etchings of your country days.

LOVE'S ENTREATIES

O foolish chick,
  don't sit there and shiver:
I hear your mother's clucking voice
inviting you
    to the nice warm place
    she has reserved
    beneath her wings
              Now run along!

Poor fearful soul,
  don't worry, fret and tremble!
Can't you hear the Savior
bidding you
    to His outstretched arms
    where love is felt
    and sins forgiven?
              Now run along! .

PRAYER OF THE SOWER

It's Spring,
Cows munch green pastures;
Birds have worms;
We dine on
    asparagus
    rhubarb
    lamb
and eat our bread three times
    a day.
Our world seems purring with content,
But in the distance I hear cries;
It is the hungry of the world
    that beg for food.

It's Spring
and time to plant my seed;
It isn't much,
But I remember well the lad
whose little loaves and fishes
fed a multitude.
So, Lord, I give the seed to Thee,
as carefully I place it in the soil.
And trust that you will multiply
    my bit
So hungry multitudes again may eat.

THE SECRET

The curious cow remarked one day
    while chewing on a cud of hay
"People are a funny brand — our farmer I can't
    understand
    his corn is wet, the mortgage's due,
    but I just never see him blue.
Even though some things go wrong,
    still he whistles out a song."

Then spoke up the wise old cat,
"That man is smart; I'll tip my hat!
    I get around....and I have found
    that people either *smile* or *frown*.
Some tarnish life with discontent,
    while other people's days are spent
    in counting all the blessings sent.
    Happiness is quite an art.
   The secret is a grateful heart."

A FARMER PRAYS

I thank You for the task I have
of planting seed.
Working hand in hand with You
is a privilege indeed.
Now I ask for Your protection,
Your warm sunshine
and Your rain
to bring, when Autumn comes,
a harvest of this grain.

                                    Amen

" *I said, Thou art my God. My times
   are in Thy hand.*"   - *Psalm 31:14, 15*

In A Stable

Oh, lowly barn,
Tonight you softly beckon me
to pause in your abode.
No decorated palace this
No dainty nursery here.

I probe the Christmas mysteries;
My voice breaks through the dusk
"Why would He leave a heavenly throne
to come to earth for this?"

Then a soft sound answers me,
a pigeon's kindly coo.
It so clearly enunciates
"For you! For you!"
And cows and kittens join the song
"For you! For you!"

"For you know the grace of our Lord Jesus Christ, that though
he was rich, yet for your sake he became poor, so that by his
poverty you might become rich."   II Corinthians 8:9

OH, FARMER FOLK

Oh, farmer folk
Let your heart sing out,
For you know what Christmas
Is all about.

'Twas to farm folk keeping watch by night
That angels came in glory bright.

You've seen a manger,
and tended sheep.
You know the quietness
when animals sleep.

It was in a barn where livestock stayed,
where cobwebs hung and donkeys brayed.
There in a dim and dusty stall
was born the Lord and King of all!

Oh farmer folk, let your voice ring out!
Tell the world what Christmas is all about!

SUPPOSE

Suppose
>   while caring for your pigs one night
>   an angel host appeared,
would you be scared?

If
>   they announced a Savior's birth
>   and invited you to see,
would you go immediately?

When
>   you had gazed upon the baby's face
>   And your heart was all aglow,
would you let your whole world know?

>   The shepherds did.

VALENTINE — COUNTRY STYLE

I'll not send a valentine
of dainty hearts and lace.
To my farmer I'll transcribe
farm symbols in its place.

It will shine with *golden sunbeams*
and sparkle with the *dew*
to tell him, "As you need these things,
so I depend on you."

'Twill have designs of *sprouted corn*
to show our love's vast size
(A rose dies with the summertime;
Grain each year multiplies.)

And finally I'll beribbon it
with *rugged baling wire*.
"May we always hang together."
— That's my valentine desire.

A FARMER'S MORNING PRAYER

Lord of my workdays
    as well as my Sabbaths,
Today I must do dangerous things.
    Make me steady!
My eyes will not always recognize dangers.
    Alert me!
In my hurrying I may become careless.
    Slow me down!

And when I grow tired and prone to accidents,
    Give me strength!
Watch over me every moment so that
    evening will find me unharmed and well.

A Wife's Prayer At Harvesttime

Father,
Bless my husband today
As he goes about his work.
Bless his *hands*, Lord,
as he uses them to bring in the harvest.
And earn our daily bread.
Keep them from clumsiness
as he works with machinery.
Keep them cautious
when they must be in dangerous places.
Keep them steady
as he controls tremendous horsepower.
All I can do is worry, Lord,
BUT Your hands are strong
and capable of guidance
and entirely trustworthy.
So I place him and his day
with You.
Make *my hands* especially loving
these busy days.
And thank you, God, for letting us
walk *hand in hand*
through the exciting days of seedtime and harvest.

                                        Amen

FARMER JOB

I didn't count on this.
It hurts to look
at fields that yesterday
stood green and tall
with promise of a fruitful fall.
In minutes all my work has come to naught.
I guess I always thought
that *hail* would pass me by.
I too would like to ask you "Why?"
But this I know......
how can I only take the good
and not accept the ill?
It is enough to be assured
You are my loving Father still.

THE PLOWMAN

There is no beauty in old fields
of stubble and dried weeds.
Each farmer knows that there can be no fruitfulness
until the plow's sharp blade
erases last year's growth;
Here only weeds will grow.
The ground is fertile
but it needs the cleansing of the plow
before good seeds can root and make this field produce.

Oh, Lord, how well You know
The fruitlessness of stubble
overgrown with weeds.
You see it in my life.
Each day I need the cleansing sweep of Your sharp plow
in full forgiveness
To uproot the sins and worldly cares
and get my heart prepared
　　to love
　　and serve.

OFF TO A VACATION!

Farewell, cows!
For several days
I'll not be at our trysting
place...
And now I ask,
"Please don't be coy
with the brand-new chores boy."
Take your stalls
without confusion.
Give your milk
without coercion.
Then happily I'll say *"adieu"*,
for the best part of the vacation
is being away from you!

THE FARMER'S PATRIOTIC HEART

This rich, black precious soil
which my plow has furrowed
I recognize not only mine,
but a piece of America.
I hold it with reverence
and am suddenly aware
that for this men fought
and died and dared.

This beautiful rich, black earth,
which my hands have worked,
is holy ground.
As a soldier of the soil, I'll tend it
for all the days I'm lent it.

NATURE ENTERTAINS

To A Pink Petunia

Tell me your secret, joyful flower
Was it a rosy dawn that showered
you with pinkish hues?
Where did you get your fragrant heart?
What alchemy set you apart
from earthy scents?
Did the sun's bright rays
act as a curling iron
to form the ruffle 'round your face?

The petunia blushed a vivid shade
"It's fun just being
what I was made to be.
My special fragrance, form and hue
come not from what I do.
I just *abide*
　　on the vine."

ROBIN ON THE LAWN

Watch me while I work.
(Or had you always heard
that God provided for the bird?)
See how I hop and hunt and peck.
Then how I tug and strain my neck
while reeling in a worm for dinner.

But God knows best.
How bored and corpulent I'd be
if I should sit upon my nest
and have the worms served up to me.

TO A MOURNING DOVE

This is your kind of day.
The lowering skies lend atmosphere
of gray and gloom
and all who hear
your joyless tune
will join with you
in your sad moanings.
Today you'll cry -
they'll sympathize.
Despondency spreads
'neath cloudy skies.
Today they'll hear
and understand
that when hearts are blue
it does demand
such utterances.
You'll sit on the branch in the
          apple tree
as concertmaster of melancholy
And soon skies
will join in with their weepings.

Requiem For A Cottonwood Tree

Now I must view
majestic, friendly you
in crude dismemberment.

These arms that welcomed
birds
and shaded herds
no longer give.

This trunk, a stately form,
that weathered storm,
no longer lives.

Thanks for beauty
you've dispensed
in quiet elegance.
Adieu, kind tree, adieu.

THE FIRST ROBIN

In Paul Revere style
it hurries from place to place,
Winging its way to city
and farm,
Relaying this message.....
"The Springtime is coming!"

DANDELIONS

Tousled yellow heads
    soon turn to white,
Then become bald
    overnight.
But even if their life span
    is brief,
They leave descendants
    beyond belief.

DAISY TALK

He loves me
He loves me not.

Forgive me, Lord.
At times I'm foolish as a child
     who measures love by daisy parts.
A disappontment, and I cry,
    "God loves me not!"
I act as if you're a fickle man
    who alternates by hourly whims;
Forgetting that your love is firm
    unchanging, sure,
More fixed than stars or sun.

All nature joins to voice this fact,
    the birds,
    the flowers,
    the trees and hills.
For who can view a daisy's face
    and state
    "He loves me not."

INSECT SOUNDS

At eventide the insects tune up
      and their orchestra begins.
They are playing their monotonous
      locust lullaby,
      saying *"Goodnight"* to the day.
Gradually the volume increases
      to a mighty hum
      that goes on and on
      and on.

But when darkness has fallen
      and quietness settles in,
And I am in my bed
      trying to sleep
I hear a cricket solo
      somewhere in my bedroom,
And the result is insomnia.

RESTLESS AUGUST

Restless August, what's your hurry?
Across the calendar page you scurry.
You rush us through the harvest time;
your metronome goes doubletime.

Put some elastic in your days.
We don't like your impatient ways.
Sweet corn. Canning. Vacation fun.
For once we'd like them leisurely done.

For when we say "good-bye" to you,
school days arrive,
summer is through!

IT'S FOR THE BIRDS!

Oh, how we stew and fuss and fume
when we redecorate a room.
Such an effort it becomes
it leaves the family in the glums.
I tell you they feel doubly blest
when nothing's needed on our nest.
But then a frightening thought occurred
— *It's an annual task for Mrs. Bird!*

CHANGE OF SEASONS

Soon our eyes will be viewing
    summer's undoing.
Her tapestries of green
    will disappear from the scene
    when leaves, grass and weed
    change to autumn tweed.

SPOKEN BY A KERNEL OF CORN

"My former shape and form is gone
    but I'm not dead.
Behold, I now live on
    IN MULTIPLE!
In giving my old self away
    I found a life of fruitfulness."

EMPTY NESTS

It isn't always summer days.
The winter comes
when bare tree silhouettes display
    empty nests.

The woods are stilled
that birdies' noisy chirps once filled
    with happy song.

These shells that once o'erflowed
where baby forms were gently stowed
    now are forlorn.

Each little birdling tried its wings
and off it flew to other Springs
    and left us all alone.

Yet even though this nest is bare
new nests are being built elsewhere
    and all is well.

THE TOUCH OF GOD

Last night this tree stood ugly,
        bare,
Dark branches jutting everywhere.
But overnight it's been transformed;
No longer can the tree be scorned.
Today I rub my eyes in glee,
"Can this be the same old tree?"
Now it's robed in garments white,
and shines and sparkles diamond-bright.
This is real. It's no illusion,
which brings me to this conclusion -
If God overnight can transform a tree,
then I'm glad that He is working on me!

THE WILD SUNFLOWER

I admit you are a pretty thing.
Your cheery face of brightest gold
    is easy to admire,
But yet, I dare not call you *flower*,
because, in fact, I know you are a weed
    and seek to overpower my fields
    and choke my crops.
Yes, you must go.
And I will plow and dig and hoe
Until my fields are rid of all your ragged
    leaves and flashy blooms.

It was a pleasant looking thing
And harmless, so I thought.
But now that it has grown
    I see I cannot call it good
for it is taking over portions of my life
that should be growing for my Lord.
Yes, I must call it by its name -
    it is a sin,
    and it must go.
Because, dear Lord, I do not want a life of
    sunflower-flashiness
    at the cost of fruitlessness.

LAND OF VARIETY

In Spring our world's a garden,
　as pretty as you please;
In Summer, a busy factory,
　where farmer and nature meet.
In Fall, it is a warehouse,
　containing our increase;
But when we reach the Winter,
　our world's a big deepfreeze!

JUST A SPARROW

Just a drab wee sparrow of little worth,
one among millions here upon earth,
but it's not forgotten of God!

It speaks to me of a Father's care
that bottles my tears
keeps track of each hair,
For if He's concerned about sparrows
then I know I'm not forgotten of God!

"Fear not, therefore, you are of more value than many sparrows."
Matthew 10:31

GOD'S SPECTACULAR

All night He worked
and as the sun came up
we gasped
to see the beauty of it all.
Each tree, each twig
was individually wrapped in white.
The sky was just
the softest hue.
Long shadows stretched
upon the dazzling snow
and little diamonds
twinkled everywhere.
Now we *"ooh"* and *"aahh"*
to see the snow
we so much dread
become a quiet
winter wonderland instead.

Family — And Other People

BABY JOE

Oh, yes, you are a lovely child,
God doeth all things well,
took Mommy's chin
and Daddy's brow,
and skillfully arranged somehow
an entirely new creation.

Sparkling there
behind blue eyes
you begin now to reveal
the *you*,
new *you*
that's baby Joe,
a unique personality.

We stand on tip-toe at your side
awaiting each discovery,
as day by day we see unveiled
the blueprint of your
individuality.

We've caught your sense of humor
by the laughings that you make.
You try so hard by hand and lip
to communicate.
And you've displayed
a generous trait
by smiles so freely given.
Your little hands,
like tendrils,
are grasping for our love.

We are filled with awe
to realize
you truly are our own......
God's gift to show us
tangibly
the greatness of His love.

GOD'S RECIPE FOR A DAUGHTER

First, some *femininity* - - one cup
Add *charm* and *beauty*; stir it up.
Then alternately in a bowl
God sifted *music* for her soul
and several teaspoonsful of *tears*,
And *happiness* to last for years.
Then with a twinkle in His eye
He said, "I think that I
    will add a *dash of tomboy*
    and *a half a cup of giggles*
    to counteract too prim a miss.
And a pound of *pep* and *wiggles*.

"Now she needs the personal touch.
Someone who will love her much.
Mother, I have chosen you
to care for her and see her through.
She must be fed, and taught and trained,
She must be kissed and loved when pained.
Oh, Mother, I've big plans for her
so use a loving hand to stir.
And don't let her be underbaked
so she'll fall flat and cause heartache.

"Teach her how to walk with me
And love other people
genuinely.
I have seen lives go amiss
because they never were taught this.
Add ruffles, ribbons, curls and bows,
and petticoats and pantihose.

And follow my instructions well
for here's a secret I will tell....
of all the lovely things I make
daughters really take the cake!"

A NEW BABY

Baby
So lately arrived from God
Still retaining a heavenly awesomeness.

Little dimpled hands
Grasping
Reaching
Feeling
    her new environment.

Baby's laughter
Made to tickle angel ears.
Baby's tears
Summon an army of willing slaves.

Baby's kiss
Sweeter than cotton candy.
And somehow she's sweeter still
When she's your own grandchild!

A PRAYER FOR BABY

Here is our baby
 a little bundle of preciousness
   and potential;
 a little heart . . . with a capacity for loving;
 a patch of virgin soil . . . waiting to be planted.
Tend her carefully, we pray.
Scatter this new ground with the seeds of Thy Word.
May it sprout and grow,
 strong and firmly rooted in Thee,
 with slender tendrils ever climbing upward,
 hungering and thirsting for righteousness,
And never knowing a time of drouth apart from Thee.
May she bask in the sunshine of Thy love
And finally blossom forth to Thy glory
 flowering with the likeness of the Rose of Sharon
 daintily scented with His love.
 A blessing to others
 and attracting souls to Thee.
Heavenly Husbandman
 only Thy green thumb upon her life
 can produce such heavenly possibilities.
      AMEN

GRANDMA'S QUILT

All the pieces in her quilt
    are scraps from her aprons and dresses.
A collage of her life
    in calicos and prints,
a thing of beauty from leftovers.

Entwined in the threads
    of the innumerable stitches
are fragments of her time —
    hours and minutes
invested and hidden in this labor of love.

Today I possess Grandma's treasure
    and I realize I'm twice blessed
For I'm warmed not only by the quilt
    but by these remnants from her days.

GRANDPA'S BARN

It was his pride and joy,
this huge structure that
added the finishing touch to his farm.
It was his ark,
filled with animals and hay
where he was Noah
tending to his creatures.
Morning and night he opened the door
to the milk cows filing into their stalls.
At milking time the cat family gathered
and patiently waited for their pans to be filled,
or a squirt of milk to be sent their way.
Then came the bucket brigade
with warm milk for the high-strung, rambunctious calves.
On the other side were the horses,
a row of muscular giants
that daily worked the fields.
He called them all by name.
And often in the pens were long-legged colts.
In those days the barn had a heart
that gave warmth and coziness to the place,
and welcomed and made each animal feel at home.
But now this building is obsolete,
the home for pigeons and mice.
Yet it is not empty
for it holds volumes of memories.
And somehow I cannot separate
my memories of Grandpa
from his barn.

MOTHER LOVE

It started out so simply
    with a tiny baby in her arms,
       and diapers,
       two o'clock feedings
       and lullabies.
As her child grew, this love grew,
    and she gave of herself —
         her lap was claimed by this little fellow,
         her kisses served as medication for both
              heart and body hurts,
         her time was not her own.
She didn't know how binding this tie had become
    until he reached boyhood
And she found this life was part of herself
         she felt pain at his pain,
         joy at his happiness,
         grief at his disobedience.
Then it was time for him to walk alone
    and she showed him *what he could be*:
         her encouragement boosted him upward,
         her prayers guided and strengthened him,
         her faith in him never faltered.
Now he is a man
    and her love has become a magnet
         with an invisible hold
         that neither party can break.
    Her love and prayers will follow her child
         even after she is gone.
         — for a mother's love and influence have no end!

TIME MARCHES ON!

I've been known as *"daughter"*, *"cousin"* and *"sis"'*
Then *"wife"* when I changed to Mrs. From Miss.
Next, I received some new attention
being called *"Mom"* gave added dimension.
Now I have reached a still higher plateau —
I became *"Grandma"* a week ago!

REMINDERS OF BABY

Baby's been to visit.
Happy memories remain.
She left her fingerprints on our hearts
And nose smudges on the pane.

WHEN BABY COMES TO VISIT

The city holds no wonders
to a girley, half past one,
  that can excite
  quite, quite like
"Grandpa's Moos".

You'll find her perched on tiptoe
beside the windowpane.
In toddler-talk she's praising,
as all day long she's gazing
  at **"Grandpa's Moos".**

But it was a different story
when she visited the barn.
She hugged us tight
in childish fright,
 for "Grandpa's Moos"
        MOOED!!!

WHERE DID THE BABY GO?

It seems but just a little while
we listened to a baby's "goos".
And coaxed a baby's smile.
Now her laughs come naturally
And she holds conversations
constantly.
Her bottles have been put away,
a fork and spoon are here to stay.
Now her rattle she's forsook
and plays with dolls and picture books.
Tiny bootees have been replaced
with wee red tennis shoes, all laced.
Behold, an energetic missy
now replaces baby Krissy.

WHAT IS A MOTHER?

A mother is a potter, molding a piece of human clay
A mother is an artist, trying to bring out on living
        canvas a useful happy personality.
A mother is a physician, whose most effective medication
        is her kisses (used for both heart and body wounds.)
A mother is a teacher, teaching right from wrong, —
        cleanliness, — responsibility — God.
A mother is a model, showing in real life how to live.
A mother is a dietitian, laundress, seamstress, nurse,
        cheerleader and referee.
A mother is God's hand. He loves and cares for His
        little ones through mothers.
For all this she is paid — not in money,
        but by the love in her children's hearts
        and the pride in their becoming happy, useful persons
        and walking with her God.

A TRIBUTE TO THE PIONEERS

Though they are gone,
these churches pointing
heavenward
speak on.
They testify of men
who had a love for God
and put Him first.
As Viking Abrahams
they came
across the prairie-land
with Sarahs by their sides.
They left the fjords
and mountain scenes behind.
Sodhouses sprouted on the plains
and from their meager stores
they sacrificed to build
a house
for Him.
Their dearest treasure
was His Word.
Though life was rough
and hardships fell,
they knelt and praised the Lord
they knew so well.
Today we still can hear their voice:
> **"We made our choice.**
> **For us and for our house,**
> **we served the Lord."**
And then we stop and wonder.....
a hundred years yonder
will history say the same
for us?

To The Graduate

You're out of breath;
the years flew by.
The climb was strenuous
but you've come so high.
Perched on this ladder
you must move with care,
for there is responsibility and danger here.
I hope you'll discover
       from the heights where you stand
that you are closer to God
       can better view the needs of man.

I know you'll be successful
       if a hot-line you install
And daily consult the *Specialist*
       whose knowledge passeth all.
Your future is unlimited
       in the profession you pursue
when you work together as colleagues . . .
       the ALMIGHTY GOD . . . and YOU!

WISHES FOR A SPECIAL TEENAGER

We watched an apple sapling grow
as it was bathed in sunshine
    and nourished by the rain.
Now it is Spring
    and we see buds.
Soon lovely blooms will cloth the tree
    and we will "*ooh*"
    and "*aaa-ah*"
    and love to linger in its fragrance.

For so it is with apple trees.
They root and grow
and then in Spring
they blossom forth and give delight.
If neither frost nor insect do molest
there will begin the satisfying times
    of beauty, fragrance, fruit.

Like this, *dear teenager*, is my wish
    for you.
Bask in the love of the heavenly Son;
Be strengthened with His Word.
Holding His protecting hand will keep you
    from the killing frosts and crippling insects
    that would hurt your life.

May the lovely blooms and fragrance of your
    life today
Develop into delicious fruits of love,
    a blessing to all those around
    and a purpose for being.
And make you God's masterpiece of beauty.

THE SEASONS OF LIFE

The apple tree perfumed
the neighborhood
and children
played beneath its boughs,
catching blossoms
in the air.
It had so much to give,
bringing joy to the world,
the loveliest tree in the woods.
It felt fulfilled
for it was Spring
and *"Spring is best!"*

A woman with salt and pepper hair
gazed on the Springtime scene
of happy children
catching blossoms
and she cried, *"Youth is best!"*
Too long she'd fussed lest breezes
blow the Spring beauty from her face and form,
as petals in the wind.
She didn't realize
the climax of the year
was Fall,
which culminates with fruitfulness,
when luscious fruit hangs on the bough.

She did not know 'tis only *TIME*
can bring the blessings of grown children,
grandchildren,
smile lines

wisdom that comes with age,
a supreme fulfillment and satisfaction
not experienced before.

For the seasons of *Fall* and *Old Age*
have rewards all their own.

THE BEGGAR

Day after day
her 1910 vintage frame
waits
beside the highway
of life.
She holds up
her empty cup,
pleading
for a drop
of attention and caring
to quench
her parched loneliness.

THE BEAUTICIAN

Her talents
and her personality blend
to draw repeat customers
to her chair.
She uses her hands
plus a listening ear
so people come away
both beautified
and befriended.

THE MAILMAN

The mailman
daily makes his rounds
from mailbox to mailbox
depositing the good,
the bad.
He cannot choose.
A letter from a loved one,
a bill
a check
bad news
junk mail.
He never knows
how he affects lives
through the mailbox.

A VOICE FROM THE CHURCHYARD

They criticized and called me Scrooge.
They did not understand.
I tell you it was love.
I loved the coins with all my heart,
Possessed them as a man a maid,
Was jealous if another's hands would grasp my gold.
Bright shining shekels beckoned me far more
Than any woman's charm,
My bank book brought me greater joy than any
    other's faithful spouse,
My love so sweetly gave to me a heady feel of power,
    security;
Her glittering beauty blinded me to other's needs.
And then the reaper came
And tore her from my arms.
Now I lie alone;
My love affair is o'er.
And I am left with tarnished hands
    a hollow rusty heart.
Night and day the faces flash
    of needy ones, of cheated ones
And there is nothing I can do in this weird world
To make amends.
Be careful what you love.

A Tumbleweed

He is a tumbleweed,
a restless wanderer,
a personage adrift,
so free and rootless that the smallest
    breeze can move him.

A whiff of wind directs his aimless way;
he'll dance to any gust
and can't resist a squall.
His lighthearted capers tell us,
"Look at me."

He will not stay around
to practice usefulness
or furnish shade for some small thing.
Impromptu living makes him say too soon,
"Goodbye and I'll be on my way."

He struts and saunters here and there
to show the world he's free
and on his own.
A spineless puppet of life's winds,
He is a tumbleweed.

SPECIAL DAYS

CELEBRATING CHRISTMAS

Lord, I can not truly celebrate
Your holy day
until I've knelt prostrate
in humble shepherd style
to worship and adore.

Oh Lord, I can not truly celebrate
Your holy day
unless it makes me imitate
the wise men who returned another way —
for seeing You must alter my ways too.

Oh Lord, let me so truly celebrate
Your holy day
that I have Mary's song
rejoicing in my heart,
that *You* are there beside me too
and I am in Your will.

A Christmas Prayer

O Lord,
    this Christmas give me a quiet heart,
    so like Mary I may ponder each significant part;
    to have time for the One who was born that day,
    to express my love in a special way.

    Give me a heart of joy this year,
    as the momentous meaning of *Your* gift becomes clear;
    to rejoice and praise Your wonderful plan —
    Immanuel — *"God makes His home with man."*

    Give me a heart with love unfurled,
    to share the reality of Your love with my world.
    Like shepherds to enthusiastically inform all I meet,
    like the Wise Men to lay my gifts at Your feet.

                        Amen

A SHEPHERD'S MEMORIES

I sat and brooded at end of day . . .
What was the world coming to, anyway?
      the price of sheep
      our land oppressed.
God had forgotten us, I guessed.

But then I heard an angel say,
"See *WHAT* has come to the world today!"
      I saw and smiled
      My world was new;
God had whispered *"I love you!"*

Is Your Heart Ready For Christmas?

Is your heart ready for Christmas?
Is it full of excitement and joy?
Now's the time to get things in order
As we wait to celebrate His birth.

Clean out the sin-webby corners;
Open yourself up to His Light.
Let Him funnel in love, warm and caring,
And make your heart sparkle with Hope.

It's time to get ready for Christmas;
Get prepared to receive your King.
For when you let your heart be His home
You'll discover the enjoyment
              that Christmas can bring.

HAVE MERCY ON US ALL

What right have I to criticize
    the Keeper of the Inn
      for giving Christ no place to stay,
When I, so absorbed in the daily race
    often leave no room for Him?

Can I pass judgment
    on Bethlehem's folk
      for placing no welcome mat,
While I admit I too am apt
    to overlook Him in my
      day-to-day living?

No words of condemnation have I
    for Herod, the ruthless king,
      who desired above all to be in control,
When I too often play the same role,
    dethroning Christ, who alone
      in my life should be reigning.

"UNTO YOU"

Like my name upon a gift tag
of a package brightly wrapped
are these personal words of Christmas.....
individual, loving, apt.

"Unto YOU the gift is given,"
sang the angels from on high.
Like the shepherds, I'll believe it
And not doubt or wonder why.

'Twas *"for ME"* the Father planned it;
'Twas *"for ME"* the Savior came.
Like the Shepherds I'll receive Him
and rejoice, give thanks, proclaim!

MARY

Mary, tell me, did you fear
To have an angel presence near?
How could you really comprehend
The mysteries that God would send?

Mary, tell me, did you thrill
At cousin Elizabeth's good will?
Did her excitement at your part
Give needed assurance to your heart?

Mary, Mary, did you cry
When Joseph thought to pass you by?
And people whispered *"What disgrace!"*
Did you dread to show your face?

Mary, did you wonder why
"blessed" should entail a sigh?
Yet reverence and joy you felt
When shepherds and the Wise Men knelt.

By faith in God you took your place
And you His glorious Will embraced.
"Behold the handmaid of the Lord,
Be it unto me according to Thy Word."

RESPONDING

Mary witnessed God's blueprint unfold
after she offered not to withhold
her life or her wishes;
In faith she concurred,
"Be it unto me according to Thy Word."

Though Mary did not understand the plan
she placed her body into God's hand.
Her answer was sure;
She never demurred,
"Be it unto me according to Thy Word."

God's Kingdom still comes
on earth today
as God's men and women willingly say,
"I'm available to do
whatever I can....
Be it unto me according to Thy plan."

Promises For The New Year

Squares dancing on the calendar pages,
    rows of unspent days,
Oh, Lord, what will these squares unfold?
You alone the answers hold.
    "My child, it is enough to say
    I will be with you twenty-four hours a day."
What if these unspent days contain
trouble, sorrow, grief and pain?
I am not strong enough to stand.
    "My child, I'll hold you by the hand.
    It is enough for you to know
    My grace will be sufficient.
    As you awaken to each dawn
    fresh and new mercies can be withdrawn.
    Anticipate the blessings there,
    for with my great love
    I've packed each square!"

THANKSGIVING LEFTOVERS

Dear Lord,
It seems that I forgot
to thank for all the little things
that brighten up my lot —
  a newsy letter in the mail
  a plant upon the sill
  sunshine dancing on the rug
  morning coffee cups to fill.
  A *"mmmm....that's good!"* at mealtime
  a freshly laundered sheet
  the happy sound of giggles
  and the patter of family feet.
For it's all these many little things
  that make my days so sweet.
Amen

A PRAYER AT BAPTISM

Our Father who art in heaven —
        Listen to our heart-applause
        — our thank-yous for this child.
        A little bit of heaven gleams
        every time he smiles.
        His chubby fingers quickly grasped
        the love-strings of our hearts.
        Everything about him
        shows how great Thou art.
        But well we know
        Thou hast reserved
        a spot just for Thine own.
        Today now fill it with Thyself
        — the Holy Spirit's home.
        Write his name
        upon Thy book
           of children
           heirs of Thine
        And add him to
        Thy family tree,
        Oh, Lord and God divine.

                for Jesus' sake,   Amen

BAPTISM PRAYER

Oh, Lord, this is a holy time
    as we gather at the font.
This precious child you gave to us
    has quickly won our hearts.
We know the love you have for him
    outweighs our earthly kind,
And today we hear your welcome words....
    "Let the little children come."

We ask your blessing on his life,
    may he run to your outstretched arms.
May he find fellowship at your knee
    as the Holy Spirit guides.
Now we stand by as your Grace is shown,
    and you make our child
        your very own.

Prayer Of The Groom's Mother

Dear Lord,
> Here they stand in your presence;
> Young,
> Radiantly happy,
> Confident.
> Be with them today . . . and when they come back down to earth again.
> Equip them with rose-colored glasses through which to discover each other's faults and weaknesses.
> Let difficulties only bring them closer to you.
> In this day of shaky marriages, bind their love together with your unbreakable cords.
> Walking side by side, may they follow after you,
> And experience the wonder of trusting in you and seeing your promises come true.
> May they give you their youth;
> May their greatest delight be in together worshiping, prayer, and serving you.
> May their home always be a welcome place for you — like that of Mary, Martha and Lazarus,
> Where each day they spend some time at your feet.
> Help me in my new role.
> Unravel any strings of possessiveness that may interfere in this new holy union.
> May I love her as my own.
> Help me not to meddle, but to do my influencing through my prayers.
> May they allow you to work out your plan for their lives.
> Make them a blessing,

salt in their environment
and lights showing forth the love of Christ.
A new home.
Smile upon it with your benediction.
That will be sufficient.

Amen.

ANNIVERSARY PRAYER

Lord, thank you for our Eden
    this niche of time and place
    where hand in hand down through the years
    we've tasted of your grace.
You've made our garden fragrant —-
    our joys you've multiplied
    by sons and daughters, plants full grown,
        grandchildren by their sides.
For all the bright prized blossoms.....
    health, friends, your love divine
    and all the little posies
    the et cetera kind.
But most of all we thank you
    for your listening ear
    and for the prayers you've answered
    year on year on year.
For permitting us each other
    for all these many days
    TO YOU DEAR HEAVENLY FATHER,
    we give bouquets of praise.
                    AMEN.

AND THE COCK CROWED

Good Friday morning was dawning
as the rooster mounted its perch.
Its cock-crow blared —
       once
       twice
       three times.
It didn't realize
its cockadoodle language
would bring weeping.
It was only meant
to awaken
 man.
. . . and it did!

Cock-a-doodle-doos
can be cheery alarm clocks,
arousing man and beast
from sleep's oblivion
to the happy consciousness
of a new day.
. . . Or according to Peter,
a shrill sad siren
opening eyes
to face past sins
. . . and the Savior.

WRITTEN IN A RAINBOW

The portals of the new year loom ahead
　　— a dark unknown.
My heart's aquiver with the fear
　　　that through this gate I may encounter
　　　trouble
　　　disappontment
　　　death or loss.
I cannot see beyond.

But then my eyes of faith
　　　behold a rainbow 'round these months.
'Tis firmly anchored to God's Word,
　　　bright spectrum of His love.

No lean year this! An arch of royal purple
　　　encircles my tomorrows with this truth —
　　　"He destined us in love
　　　to be His sons through Christ." (Eph. 1:5)
I'll walk through each new day
　　　aware that I'm a daughter of the King.

Why should I dread, when looking up I see the
　　　rosy glow of Romans 8:28?
　　　"In everything God works for good
　　　with those who love Him."
Our Father's guarantee that all will come out best!

I need not falter, though my path be strange
　　　when in neon brilliance these words shine —
　　　"I will instruct thee and teach thee
　　　In the way that thou shalt go." (Psalm 32:8)

How can I hesitate if One so great will guide my way?

Then welcome brand new year!
When rainbowed with His faithfulness
    you give three hundred sixty-five
    new opportunities
    . . . to walk with God!

AFTER EASTER

Is it back to old routines? Just living on the fading joys
of Easter morn?

'Twas after Easter that excitement reigned
as followers beheld *HIS* face;
at unexpected times and place,
LO, HE WAS THERE!

Today the *LIVING* Savior
breaks into our days
at unexpected moments and in many
different ways
to remind us . . .
"LO, I AM WITH YOU ALWAY!"

ASCENSION DAY

Once again He was *home* at His Father's side.
Earth had done its worst; He'd been crucified.
Now the angels' announcement was clear and plain
    "As He disappeared in the clouds, you'll see
    Him coming again."

So be busy in His harvest; Keep an eye on the sky.
Each day be ready, for His return draweth nigh!

ARE YOU WAITING FOR HIS APPEARING?
                          II Timothy 4:8

COME BEFORE HIS PRESENCE WITH
THANKSGIVING

Lord of all the earth and sky,
the great *"I AM'* who can satisfy.
Thank You for Your creation.
    the sweetness of the lark's bright song,
    the beauty of an oak so strong,
    the power that makes day break each morn,
We thank You, Great Creator.

O Lord, who has created man,
And designed the family in Your plan,
For this we thank you.
    for love that blossoms in the home,
    for precious children that You loan,
    to need and be needed by someone,
For this we thank You.

O Lord, who gave to man a soul
And provided a way to make him whole,
For this we thank You.
    to know the sweetness of Your grace,
    the forgiveness that our sins erase,
    the joy of Your presence through our days,
For this we thank You.

And one day when our faith is sight,
To be in Your presence, what delight
At last to be able to give thanks aright,
Then, Oh Lord, we will thank you forever.

**"Let us come into his presence with thanksgiving; let us make
a joyful noise to him with songs of praise!**   **Psalm 95:2**

Prayer For The New Year

O Lord, my God.....
Were I a lady Solomon
with any wish to choose,
Before the new year just ahead
I'd make this one request,
    'HELP ME TO LEAN.'

I stand upon this threshold strange
and feel I'm but a child;
Yet one who leans need not be strong,
Be my support and guide,
    'O HELP ME LEAN.'

Yes, leaning is a simple thing,
Yet my independent self
may lead me from the path
Thy Loving will has planned.
So stay close by
through each succeeding day
And help me, Lord, to daily lean on Thee.

                Amen

THE HOSPITAL

Factory of healing
beehive of activity
the white-frocked female's domain.

A busy depot
where new little boys and girls
make their first stop
and many bodies get back
on the right track.

A repair stop for many
. . . and the last stop for some
where passengers wear basic back-tied clothes
that are often accessorized
with bandages, clips and casts
And lunch on pills and capsules.
Where pain is soothed with a needle
and you are pulsed and blood-pressured
day and night.

You may have to enter
the "arena of no memories"
where green garmented men and women
battle for your health
with scalpel and suture.

And you will always have the memory
of the tasteless thermometer
. . . and the deliciousness
of plain ice water.

Nurses . . . the efficient cogs in the wheels
that wake you in the morning
and tuck you in at night,
Their smiles give encouragement,
their words bring assurance
and they have the amazing ability
To handle bodies
of all dimensions.

Here your eyes are opened to fellow sufferers
. . . in worse shape than you,
and your heart thumps with thanksgiving
when health is close at hand
and you bid "Farewell"
resolving to bring cheer to others
who travel this horizontal trail.

For you have learned
that being remembered
is the magic medicine
that heals and strengthens the heart
. . . no matter what the malady.

"UNTO THEE O LORD DO I LIFT UP MY VOICE"

MY SONG

I will sing to God, my Father,
    who has always cared for me.
    Before I was......
    He held me in His heart
    and planned so perfectly
    my *hows* and *wheres* and *whens.*

I will sing to Jesus Christ, my Lord,
    who when He hung upon the tree
    bore *my* sins
    and on that day I know He thought of me.

I will sing of God, the Holy Ghost,
    who from childhood guided me
    into the knowledge of my Lord,
    and now makes His home in me.

Great God in three.....
    today *your* mighty hand holds mine
    and offers fellowship divine.

God of my tomorrows
    still stay near,
    and some day bring
    to sweet fruition
    the longed-for meeting
    face to face
    of Thee
    . . . and me.
                    Amen

HAVE A GOOD DAY!

When you open your eyes each morning,
    turn heavenward your face.
Present to God your sacrifice,
    — *your sentences of praise.*
As priests who laid burnt offerings
    on the altar every day,
So bring your *living* sacrifice.
    GOOD days begin that way!

"My voice you will hear in the morning. In the morning I will
direct it to You . . . and I will look up."   Psalm 5:3

WHAT SHALL I RENDER UNTO THE LORD FOR ALL OF HIS BENEFITS?

Ps. 116:12

My heart is full
Blessings abound.
My whole being is yearning to expound
     my thanksgiving;
But words are not enough.
What can I render unto the Lord
    for all of His benefits?

He can't be repaid.
Grace came to bless.
But I am searching for avenues to express
    my thanksgiving,
because words are not enough.
What can I render unto the Lord
    for all of His benefts?

Just bloom where you're planted,
That's all that He asks.
He'll furnish the fragrance; your task
    is to be available
And spread His Kingdom to your spot
    on earth.
This you can render unto the Lord
    for all of His benefits.

RECEIVING THE WORD

Sometimes your Word comes as a pink dawn,
    filtering into my remembrance
    and turning my night into day.
At times it arrives like lightning
    striking at a vital part of me
    and the message hits home.
Often it falls as a summer rain
    on my parched and thirsty heart,
    and I am refreshed and revived.
Frequently it settles like a sunset
    and gives my whole world a golden glow
    even clouds take on the color of your love.
O Lord, I am glad that I am yours
    and that you reach me
    through your Word.

BEAUTIFUL FEET

The Word needs feet to reach the world.
        obedient feet to spread the news to people
            who have never heard.
        willing feet who quickly go
            to explain the Word to those who know.
        loving feet who linger near
            and share the Good News because they care.

Angels watch and wish to go
        but the Father would not have it so.
God in His almighty plan
        chose to send it man to man.
Expectant hearts now wait to greet
        the Good News that comes by human feet.

One day when our race is won
        may we hear the Lord's "Well Done!"
What added joy when our Savior we meet
        to hear Him whisper . . .
        "You had beautiful feet."

AWED BY GOD

To think that God would give His son
For mankind — sinners everyone
. . . *But He did!*

To think that God would take the care
To listen to each faltering prayer,
. . . *But He does!*

To think that God would be concerned
And even watch the little birds,
. . . *But He does!*

To think that God would want our love
And yearn for us from heaven above,
. . . *But He does!*

MY PERSONAL PSALM OF PRAISE

I love you, O Lord, my Rock.
You are always there, solid, faithful and dependable
— *not like the shifting sands that no one can build on.*
You are a strong shelter when life is difficult.

When I came face to face with threatening illness
I called on you and you assured me you were there,
working all things out for good.
FOR THIS YOU ARE WORTHY OF PRAISE..

When I am concerned for my dear ones,
and tremble at the dangers they face,
I call on you.
You tell me not to be anxious,
that they are safe in your fortress.
FOR THIS YOU ARE WORTHY OF PRAISE.

You are my resting place in the shadow of the Rock,
— away from the heat and stress of the day.
Here you put my heart at rest and peace covers my life.
Praise be to my Rock,
my security.
I will sing your praise before men.

PRAYER

after reading Psalm 139: 23,24

My heart is rough and homespun —
    an ordinary kind,
It's much the worse for wear and tear;
    to sin it is inclined.
Oh, see the strained relationships,
    the spots where love's worn thin,
    frayed edges of my patience
    the pockets full of sin.
I know it isn't worthy
    Your label to display,
But take this tattered garment
    and work on it today.
Oh, Thou Master Mender,
    reweave each ugly tear;
Make it the loving raiment
    a child of Thine should wear.

THE SHEPHERD PSALM

Of the Psalms, the 23rd is the favorite of them all. It has a message for everyone — the child, — the youth — the adult and the aged.

LITTLE CHILD, how blessed
To be the Shepherd's lamb.
Tenderly He holds you to His gentle breast,
Little child, you trust Him, and readily accept Him;
You shall never want.

Oh YOUTH, you dream of pastures green
Where flows the cool and bubbly stream.
But can you find the way without a guide?
The Shepherd waits to lead you there,
To choose your way, your work, your mate,
In your own wisdom you may find
        a thistle patch
        a stagnant pool.
Oh, tender youth, you need Him
To guide your teenage days.

Dear ADULT, you have found your place........
        a home to keep
        a job to do.
But daily life can be so hard
So let your Shepherd see you through
        each day,
        each hour.
Then humdrum tasks are glorified.
Oh, burdened one, just lean on Him.
Your soul He's promised to restore.

In paths of righteousness He'll lead
Forevermore.

Old PILGRIM, you've walked by His side
For many miles,
He's proved His faithfulness!
Now you have time to reminisce
    on blessings past,
    His kindnesses,
And sing, "My cup o'erflows."
Your confidence in Him is strong.
You know what future days will be . . .
    goodness and mercy there you'll see
And then you'll dwell with Him.

Weak DYING FRIEND, fresh courage take.
Your Shepherd cares from birth to death.
When walking through the valley dark
You need not fear. He definitely will be there.
If you would cling, then cling to Him.
Your Shepherd then will hold your hand
And take you to His better land.

"Good Shepherd, many thanks to Thee,
For being our sufficiency
Through all our days!"

Valentine Prayer

Give us a denim love
    that's tough enough to stand the strain
    of everydays and still remain;
    with warmth to melt our selfishness;
    strong enough to bear financial stress.
A love that's comfortable and brings
    enjoyment in the little things.
True, genuine and honest to the core,
    . . . *a denim love*
    that's guaranteed to wear
    and each year grow better
    than before.

                                  Amen

THE GIFT OF MEMORIES

How lusterless would be our days
    without the gift of memories.
They are the precious threads that weave
    the Present with the Past,
      both sweet and bitter moments
      that can last and last and last.
Every memory in some way
    can embellish the tapestry of *TODAY*.
Thank you, Lord, for darker strands
    the times that were so hard,
      that remind of lessons You have taught
      when we were hurt and scarred.
Shining golden filaments
    are woven here and there,
    remembrances when You've been close,
    . . . the Mary-times
    . . . the answered prayers.
As we savor these times once more,
    life is given an added dimension
    and we are blessed because of them
    often beyond comprehension.

"DON'T YOU KNOW THAT I MAKE BUTTERFLIES?"

My child,
you lie in a cocoon
of your own making,
bound 'round and 'round by chords
of selfishness, habits and fears.
In its depths you are
cut off from **me**
and your fellowmen.
Oh, let me set you free!
I can loosen your bonds
so your wings can unfold
and you can take beautiful flight
on the currents of my love
and gently touch others.
Don't you know that I make butterflies?

WHERE ARE THE NINE?

from Luke 17:17

The sad voice of Jesus echoes down through time,
"Were there not ten? Then where are the nine?"
Were they so busy enjoying new life
They forgot the Giver and went home to their wives?

The nine were His people
But they acted so rude
While He stood there and waited
For some gratitude.

I want to be numbered with the unlikely *"one"*—
The healed Samaritan leper, who
    came back on the run.

God blesses today, and the situation is the same.
Too often the blest ones called by His Name
Take His benefits for granted
And this to their shame,
While the unlikely ones, the sick, poor and lame,
    are the ones at His feet,
Thanking, praising His name.

Can you still hear Him asking to all of mankind,
    "Were there not ten I blessed?
    Where are the nine?"

I HEARD MY NAME

God's advances could not penetrate
The shell around my heart,
Till he placed in his bow
Isaiah forty-three
And aimed each verse at me.

"I have called you by name" was the first arrow
    to find its mark (Isa. 43:1)
And crack the hard surface;
I knew God loved the world,
But that day he made it personal.
I heard *my* name
And listened.

"Fear not!" he said. (Isa. 43:1)
I had held God at arm's length
Because I was afraid to let him reign.
But today he came with such personal love
I wanted more.

He whispered, *"You are mine."* (Isa. 43:1)
Every heart wants to belong to someone
Or something.
And I discovered
My Master
And Redeemer.
Purchased at Calvary,
I was his costly possession.

As one who would not leave his loved
one's side, I heard him promise, *"I will be
with you."* (Isa. 43:2)

Through deep waters
And fiery trials,
Through good days and bad.
As he was with Daniel,
Shadrack, Meshach, and Abednego,
And Moses,
And Mary.

*"You are precious in my sight....
    and I love you"* (Isa. 43:4)
pierced my shell in two.
All the pieces fell from me.
My bare thirsty heart
Drank of this redeeming love.
And life was new
And abundant.
For he gave purpose to my life.

"I have created you for my glory." (Isa. 43:7)
An earthen vessel
For him to dwell in
And transform.
A Savior to love
A Master to serve.
A God to glorify.

"You are my witnesses. (Isa. 43:10)
Know me.
Trust me.
Share my first-name-basis love
So other thirsty hearts may know
And drink
And live."
I heard him call my name.
That day my heart was conquered.

THE FATHER'S LOVE

I placed *"I love yous"* in my Word
    from Genesis to Jude.
I desired each soul upon my earth
    know of its magnitude.

And then I acted out my love
    — my love for sinful man —
One black Friday when MY Son
    carried out the plan.

I let Him die upon the cross,
    a sacrifice for sin,
That He could be THE WAY — the bridge
    to bring my children in.

Oh, come to Him
Our love to know.
My Father-heart yearns for you so.

THERE'S MORE!

(according to Ephesians 1)

For years I'd been content to grovel in defeat,
    clutching salvation to my breast,
    not knowing there was more.
One day breezes of the Spirit blew
    and through the Word I caught a glimpse of it —
    the victorious life.

There stood the Resurrected Christ, inviting
    "Child, arise!
    Arise and walk the heavenly paths with me.
    Inhale the exhilarating atmosphere of
        Grace and Love
        until your heart beats strong.
    Arise, and look to Me,
        then stronger than a magnet's pull
        you'll feel the greatness of God's power
        at work in you
        and know the riches of your
        glorious inheritance
        and hope.
    Your days of struggling can be o'er,
    I am the Victory,
        Come . . .
        relax . . .
        and sit with me
            in heavenly places."

A MESSAGE FROM THE MASTER

Take heart, bereaved one;
It is I.
Though you are swamped by waves of grief
and fear you can't withstand the gale,
look up, for I am here.
    I understand;
    I too have wept.
Now take my hand
and we will walk across the waves
    (it's possible with Me.)
And I will get into your boat
and calm will come.
Then I, Myself, will comfort you,
for am I not the stiller of the storm?

HE WHO HAS EARS TO HEAR,
LET HIM HEAR!

Do you have a hearing problem?
Are God's words indistinguishable and blurred?
He's been trying to tell you of His love,
    how He wants to guide you from above;
    how He wants to instruct you with His commands;
    to converse with you,
    walk hand in hand,
And you don't even know what you're missing!

Dig out from your ears all that blocks His voice —
    the waxes of self-centeredness,
    pride and wrong choice;
    the dirt and dust of worldly cares;
    the busyness that keeps you from prayer.
Oh, make your hearing keen again
    so you can hear and understand
    each word that He whispers sweet and clear
For God delights in a listening ear.

DON'T EVER TAKE SALVATION LIGHTLY!

That night in the garden, He sweat drops of blood
as He struggled with the assignment
    that would bring us good.
On His knees He agonized in Gethsemane,
        — Oh, don't ever take salvation lightly!

As He hung on the cross in pain and disgrace,
even bereft of His Father's face,
willing to accept sin's penalty in our place,
        — please, never, never take it lightly!

"It is FINISHED!" He cries.
It's a victory shout.
"I've fought your battle, I've paid your price.
I love you, my friend,
        — but please, don't ever take it lightly!"

"I'M COMING TO YOUR HOUSE TODAY"

Has life got you cornered
        and up in a tree?
Is your heart heavy?
        Then listen to me.

Jesus is here and He's
        calling to you,
*"Come down from your perch,
        my acquaintance renew.*

*We'll fellowship together
        and I'll be your friend.
Nothing is hopeless
        when on Me you depend.*

*You're special to Me
        so don't tell me "Nay".
Happiness is waiting . . .
        I'm coming to your house today!"*

THE PEOPLE GOD USES

God has His plans
  And hand-picks people to carry them out.
People like Mary . . .
  God wouldn't entrust His beloved Son
  to just anyone.
  She must be loving and humble
  But most of all she must be willing.
  . . . *and she was* . . .
  She gave up her own rights and plans for His
  when she said, "*Be it unto me according to Thy*
Word."

Or like Joseph . . .
  God wouldn't choose just any man.
  He didn't need a leader.
  To carry out His plans He needed someone
      sensitive to *His* leading
      and quick to obey.
  One who would stand in the background
      and be a support and provider.
      . . . *and Joseph was* . . .
  He gave up his own ambitions
      and even left His own country
  To carry out God's plans
      because in his heart he had said,
      "*Thy will be done.*"

TODAY God has His plans
  and hand-picks people to carry them out.
He still looks for *the humble* and *the willing,*
  and those *sensitive to His leading.*

114

When He taps *you* on the shoulder
    . . . or *me*
    and then bends down His ear for our response,
If it's the same as Joseph or Mary's . . .
    then He can use us too!

BURDENED

My dream . . .
It haunts me.

I saw the world
Through God's lenses:
*every man did what was right
in his own eyes . . .*
and who wanted God's plumb line?

I wanted to shake them
And wake them
Out of their syncopated beat,
self-gratification
new morality
To see the handwriting on the wall.

It was urgent.
I had to tell them!
But with the tortuous effort of a dreamer
I could not speak
I could not shout.
And the world rushed madly on!

Then I awoke . . .
tormented
For I had seen His message . . .
"Behold I come quickly!"
While they did not know.
And what if it is just about time?

"Surely I am coming soon." - Revelation 22:20

THE CARPENTER AND THE TREE

A tree grew in Judea
Reaching upward straight and tall.
And in the sun and rain it dreamed . . .
    of a carpenter's hands
    so kind and skilled
who someday with his tools and nails
    would fashion of it
    a thing of beauty.
    Perhaps a bed
        a chair
    where man could rest his frame.

The day arrived.
A carpenter's kind hands
    carried it away.
But it was up the hill of Calvary
    that nightmarish day.
Cruel hands had made of it a cross
    and the day was dark
    and the nails were sharp.
Now in ugliness and shame
    this tree held *the carpenter's* frame.

But the tree of Judea did not know
    that in *Christ's* hours of pain
This carpenter was building still —
    fashioning from this tree a bridge
    for all mankind to walk to God.

HURRY UP, PLEASE, IT'S TIME!

In the church she waits,
    "Hurry up, please. It's time!"
Her heart pounds with excitement and joy,
Soon hopes and dreams will be fulfilled.
She straightens her veil,
picks up her bouquet
and begins her walk down the aisle.
It's just about time
    to become his bride.

The jailer approaches the prisoner's cell.
    "Hurry up, please. It's time!"
Time to take the walk to the Judge's bench
To stand alone
with a heart of dread.
It's just about time
    to be sentenced and judged.

God's handwriting on the wall . . .
"Yea, surely I come quickly"
    "Hurry up, please. It's time!"
Each heart must now make some response.
It's just about time
to meet Him
    as Bridegroom
    — or as Judge.

In God's Time

"Ye ought always to pray and not to faint." Luke 18:1

I came in urgency and asked,
the answer did not come.
Days turned to months and months to years,
I questioned *"Why?"* and *"When?"*

"Wait" is a foreign word to me,
for in this push-button world I live
I want immediate results.
How can I wait and not lose heart?

Then down the avenues of time
these words of God resound:
"It may seem slow, but wait for it;
The just shall live by faith." (Habakkuk 2:3,4)

Man may be master of machine,
But the *"whens"* belong to God.
So be content in this assurance . . .
  HE IS ABLE
  HE IS WISE
And quietly in His love await
  GOD'S TIME.

YOU ARE A BUILDER

(Matthew 7:24-29)

You are a BUILDER . . .
Your life will be the building
    so take care.
Each day you add a section -
    each word, each deed, each goal.
Both godly choice and selfish act
    will show up in the whole..
One day the winds will come,
    the heavy rain,
The times of difficulty, grief and pain.
Will your house stand?
    It will depend . . .
Have you a Rock foundation and call
    Jesus . . . *Savior? . . . friend?*
Or did you choose a foolish plan
    by building on the shifting sand?

YOURS FOR THE TAKING!

God showed me his treasure chest of promises
And said, *"Help yourself!"*

I lifted the lid to all this wealth
And in excitement grasped the treasure that shone
    the most.
It was the pearl of great price —
    "He that hath the Son hath life" (I John 5:12).
I slipped it on my finger and wore it through my
    everydayness.
Its constant sparkle gave my life joy.
It was the promise of eternal life.

He noticed I was lonely and afraid,
And gave me this promise —
    "I will never leave thee, nor forsake thee" (Heb. 12:5b).
And when I picked it up,
It was a cloak to wear on my shoulders,
And, oh, it kept me warm and comfortable,
Even in sorrow, disappointment and death.
It was the promise of his presence.

I was ashamed as I looked at my hands
So dirty and stained.
In his chest I found a costly ointment —
    "If we confess our sins, he is faithful and just, and will
    forgive our sins and cleanse us from all unrighteousness."
                                          (I John 1:9)
Every application left me with the clean fragrance of
    peace,
And the healing of Calvary.
This was the promise of his forgiveness.

On my back I was carrying a heavy pack
Of worries and cares.
"I do not like to see this," he said.
And brought out of his treasure chest a purse,
Richly embroidered with these words —
> *"Casting all your care upon him; for he careth for you."*
>> (I Pet. 5:7)

And, behold, in its bottom was a large opening!
When I drop my cares in there
They disappear.
He follows behind and picks them up
And solves them for me.
This was the promise of his providential care.

My feet were sore from the rough and stony road
And I could not go on.
He knew the way I took
And his sympathetic voice said, "Try this —
> *"My grace is sufficient for you"* (2 Cor. 12:9)

I stepped into this rugged pair of boots
That were soft as slippers to my feet.
They carried me over all terrain
In all kinds of weather.
And I came safely through
For this was the promise of his strength.

Ahead the way was very dark;
I could not see the end.
From the chest a luminous promise glowed —
> *"In my Father's House are many mansions; I go to*
> *prepare a place for you."* (John 14:1,2)

He placed this light in my hands,
And it shed a beam into my future.
It was the promise of heaven.

Then he showed me the most precious gift of all —
The victor's crown.
Too beautiful for words!
A laurel wreath,
    emerald leafed
    gold filigreed
    and diamonded.
"I will inscribe your name on it," he said.
"And keep it for you."
Yes, it was the best promise of all —
    *"Be thou faithful unto death and I will give thee the
    crown of life."* (Rev. 2:11b)

In tears I fell at his feet.
"All this wealth is too much for me!"
But he answered, "He who did not spare his own Son, will
    he not also give you all things?
Use my promises for a life more abundant!"

And from a heart that had tasted the riches of Christ,
And knew there was more to come,
I humbly whispered,
    "Thank you, God."

THE MESSAGE

Everywhere I look I see
LOST SHEEP . . .
bewildered
scared
lonely
wounded and
showing the effects of their wanderings.
They act as if their shepherd is dead.

Hurry and tell them the good news of Easter . . .
Their Good Shepherd Lives!
He lives!   He lives!

THE CHEERING SECTION

"Keep Going!" Moses calls.
"Stay with it!" Abraham commands.
Men from the cloud announce
the reward is worth the race.

"Hold on!" Jacob shouts.
"Take Heart!" Joseph commends.
Men from the cloud have found
HE'S faithful to the end.

"Wherefore seeing we also are compassed about with so great a cloud of witnesses, let us lay aside every weight, and the sin which doth so easily beset us, and let us run with patience the race that is set before us, LOOKING UNTO JESUS, the author and finisher of our faith."
— Hebrews 12:1,2

THE PRAYER OF A LUKEWARM HEART

Oh Lord,
How can I get the heartfires burning brightly
    once again?
They died so gradually
I didn't realize the flame was almost gone.
Now I recall the days of cozy fellowship
when the new fire was all aglow
and I was revelling in your nearness.
Oh Lord, you yearn for a warm heart in me
and so do I.
This tepid one brings me no joy.

And then *HE* said,
"Just feed the fire with thoughts of my
    great love for you.
Keep adding them at times throughout the day.
Shake down the ashes of past works
    and past priorities.
Then fan the sparks with honest talks with me,
    confession, praise and thanks.
— AND IT WILL BURN AGAIN.

Oh, let your very self be fuel
for in the burning I am near.
A heart aflame with love for me
will warm the persons near to you
And be *my witness* here on earth."

WHAT IS FAITH?

Into her father's lap she climbed
with a weighty problem on her mind.
While being engulfed in loving arms
she questioned, "Daddy, what's *FAITH?*"

> *'Oh, God, she needs wiser lips than mine"*
> *to explain this profound truth divine."*

My child, to have it simply put,
it's like you and me — only so much more!
. . . like coming to me with your questions
    and knowing I'll listen;
. . . bringing your problems
    and expecting me to solve them;
. . . running to my lap
    and knowing I'll never turn you away.

So it is with faith in God.
It's coming to your heavenly Father
    with your questions and problems,
    climbing into His lap
    and letting yourself be enfolded in the
    arms of His love.
Just like you and me — only so much more!

MY DAY IN THE ARMY

The bugle blared
 morning reveille
I turned over and decided to sleep in
 and go without breakfast,
  while others ate the special food,
  the meat and milk of the Word.
My orders — *"Meet with your commanding officer"*,
 were overlooked.
I busied myself
 polishing my shoes
 making my bunk.
Then came the call to battle —
  But I had misplaced my sword of the spirit,
  My helmet was rusty,
  And my gospel armour was in mothballs.
So I gave them a dollar and told them to get someone
 to take my place.
I watched them march out . . . with empty places
 in the ranks.

By then I was weak and tired
and I took a long nap,
After which I put on my dress uniform and
 paraded up and down the streets
So people could see what a fine soldier I was.

Now the day was almost gone;
the sound of Taps
fell on my ears.
The men were coming home from the conflict
singing their battle song

"I have fought the good fight,
I have finished my course
I have kept the faith."
The encounter had been intense.
Some were wounded and bruised
and some had given their lives.
The Man that led had nail-scarred hands.
All day He had fought by their side.

And He looked at me . . .
  and the cock crowed
  and I went out and wept
  for I had only been playing soldier.

I'll Hold Your Hand

When days of suffering plague you,
    more pain than you can stand,
I'll be there by your bedside,
    holding your right hand.

When fears rise up like specters,
    engulfing your heart and mind,
Remember I'm right beside you . . .
    you'll find peace with your hand in mine.

The day grief overtakes you
    and life's ways you don't understand,
Let me be your comfort;
    I'll never let go of your hand.

In the everydays of your journey
    we'll have fellowship so grand.
You'll experience an extra special joy
    . . . *for I'll be holding your hand!*

"Nevertheless I am continually with Thee. Thou dost hold my right hand."

—*Psalm 73:23*

THE CONFRONTATION

"Do you love me?"
"Why, certainly," I said,
and chattered on about
my busyness
my plans.

"Do you *really* love me?"
His eyes met mine.
Uncomfortably I took the time
To look within,
and, lo, there was no room for Him.
My heart was filled with self . . .
my choice
my ways,
my things.
In shame I bowed my head.

"Do you love me?"
Again I heard His voice.
I saw the nail prints in His hands,
and slowly raised my eyes to His
and honestly confessed
"Oh Lord, You know my heart."
He smiled and took my hand
and now I listen for *HIS* choice.
                    HIS plans.

FAITH COMETH BY THE WORD

I read of a God who created the world,
    the sun, mountains, oceans, flowers and birds,
    man and woman, fields, trees and herds.
What a feat!
          . . . and I believed it.

I read of His Son who for thirty-three years
    revealed His Father as He walked among men,
    inviting . . .
    "Come unto me, ye heavy laden."
          . . . and I yearned to know Him.

I read of the sad condition of man:
    "All have sinned and come short.
    To be good . . . no one can!"
          . . . and I knew in my heart it was true.

I read of His Son dying on the tree
    a sacrifice for sin there at Calvary.
Then I realized He went through all this for me.
    SUCH LOVE!
          . . . and I believed *IN HIM!*

THE PRUNING PROCESS

Be patient with me, Father.
I see what you're trying to do;
But it hurts....
And my old self wants to rebel,
Proving I need this, it's true.

With my lips I have prayed,
"Thy will be done."
Now give me the strength
to submit . . .
For only when this struggle subsides
can raw tender tissues knit.

Be patient with me, Father,
though my lips may cry out or sigh,
For this heart desires
a cleansed branch to be,
Producing choice fruit for Thee.

TOO BUSY?

No time for ME, sin-burdened soul?
Please come, pour out your wrongs
And I will wash you clean,
       . . . then you'll have *PEACE*.

No time for ME, sad, lonely one?
Come, sit with Me and I
 will tell you how I care for you.
Am always by your side,
       . . . and you'll feel *LOVED*.

No time for ME? Oh, don't you know
I yearn to have you come?
And as you raise
your thanks and praise,
       . . . then you'll know *JOY*.

CONVERSATIONS
WITH EVE

Just Like You

Once I was flesh and blood
     like you.
I made a man's heart skip a beat,
Held babies on my knee.
Knew joy and sorrow,
     heartache and regret.
I blazed the trail of womanhood
     as wife
     and mother,
     grandma too.
I lived and breathed
     and laughed
     and cried.
I was a real live woman
     just like you.

LOVE AT FIRST SIGHT

I awoke to life
       and he was there.
He took my hands
       and tenderly he
       stroked my hair.
He drew me
       in his arms
and it was no surprise
to find I belonged
       there by his side.
. . . *then love was born in Paradise.*

Adam's Psalm Of Love

This is it!
Oh God, you've given me delight.
This creature you have formed
is wonderful!
Her dainty beauty
warmth of heart
        companion,
        playmate,
        helper,
        wife.
I want to shout
I want to praise
      Hurray!
      Whoopee!
It is the end of lonely days.

ADAM'S ODE TO EVE

You were the ingredient that
      made Eden Paradise.
Before you came
this garden was a zoo
      of animals and birds
a horticultural display
      of flowers and herbs
which could not fill the lonely
      spaces in my heart.
And then you came . . .
      someone to understand
          communicate
          and love
And I was satisfied.

THE SCAR

He loved to tease
        and call me *"Rib"*,
And there upon his naked flesh
        was proof.
Each time I saw the scar
it spoke of my creation
on the day
the Lord from Adam's side
prepared me for his man.
        bone of his bone
        flesh of his flesh
But for that scar I would not be.

Centuries later
on another's flesh
were Calvary scars.
But for those wounds I would not live eternally.

A WOMAN'S INFLUENCE

Don't underestimate
your words
your deeds
your love.
You are the lodestar
of your universe
And can cause
blessing
or a curse.
I KNOW.
My husband listened
to my voice
and ate
forbidden fruit.

THE FORBIDDEN

In introspect
        it looked so sweet
                delicious
                satisfying.
My mouth was watering for its fruit.
But with each bite
I found it bitter
        ugly
        poisonous.
And never could I get the taste
of sin
out of my mouth.
For I discovered
I had eaten of the worm
together with the fruit.

NOTHING TO WEAR

I wince as I recall
the moments following *the Fall*
when suddenly I realized my plight
and grabbed the only things in sight —
      fig leaves.

"The Seed of the Woman Shall Crush . . ." -Gen. 3:15

The weight of sin was more than I could bear
until I heard those words,
    (for John 3:16 was written there.)
It gave me strength to undertake
For then I knew
there would be better days.

FURS

I wore the first fur
  but took no delight in it.
You wear your furs with pride,
  a mark of your prosperity.
I wore mine to hide
  my shame and spiritual
  poverty.

IF

If I had been busy
  counting the blessings
  in my lovely world
I would not have had
  time to drool
  over forbidden fruit.

GOD CALLING YET

He called our names
and waited for response.
We uttered not a word.

Our love for Him
had turned to fear
and so we cowered there
behind the sin curtain.

And still He calls
and each must choose
to walk with Him
or hide
behind the sin curtain.

MOVING DAY

I turned and took
       one last
       longing
       look
through tearfilled eyes.
How do you say goodbye
to Paradise?
We packed our memories
and
hand in hand
we stumbled through the gate,
two strangers in a hostile land
where we would always bear
the stigma —
       "THE EVICTED".

THE FIRST BABY

When I first beheld him
I was filled with awe;
The breath of heaven fresh
        upon his brow.
I whispered, *"Adam, see....*
        a human replica
        made in the likenesses
        of you and me."
With God's help, we have a son.
See the great thing God has done!

MINIATURES

I'd seen a bud upon the rose,
        similar form and color,
        the resemblance shows.
I'd seen a newborn kitten,
        faint *"meouws"* and tiny frame
        mother and kitten were much the same.
Now I look upon small toes,
        a tiny mouth and little nose,
        . . . .a human miniature like us!
And I can say, "This is my child,
but, oh my God,
this is Your Masterpiece."

"And God Said
"HAVE DOMINION OVER . . ."

In Eden
it was easy . . .
      flowers bloomed
      and animals obeyed.
But afterwards
we spent a lifetime struggling
      with weeds and bugs,
      and stubborn mules
      angry oxen and makeshift tools
while trying to fulfill this one
command . . . *"Have dominion over . . . "*

DEATH

O God,
how can I understand
this mystery called death?
My heart is torn
by mother's grief.
I speak —
there's no response.
Already I am lonely for his voice,
his smile.
I see his body
But he is not living there.
My son.
My son.

MY GARDEN

A little plot . . .
       of lilies
       roses
       and forget-me-nots.
Year after year
down on my knees
I labored there
       trying to satisfy
       my appetite
       for beauty
whetted
       long ago
in lovely Eden.

TO SING OR COMPLAIN

I grumbled through a rainy day,
    my body tired and full of fears
when there broke through into
    my world
a lark's sweet song.
I paused and watched the little bird.
It raised its wee head heavenward
    and happiness spilled out.
"How can you sing? You little thing?
Your world is difficult as mine — to search for food
to weather storms, to live with danger prowling
    'round.
What is the key?"
    "Look upward, Eve, and you will know
    that God is in control.
    Just let His praises fill
    your soul,
    And you will also
    have a singing habit."

A Bedtime Story

Once upon a time . . .
there was a garden fine.
The trees were laden with their fruit.
The flowers blossomed fragrant there.
And do you know?
       the lamb and lion rested
           side by side
       and there was neither fear
           nor strife.
       And no one hurt
       and no one cried
       and no one ached
       and no one died.
And everything was fair
and WE were there —
       IN THE GARDEN.